PREFACE

During the days of slavery, many of the slave masters took actual credit for their slaves' creative ideas. As a result, Black scientists and inventors were not always able to obtain patents. Patents are documents that give legal ownership to one's idea or product.

It should be understood that, throughout time, Black scientists and inventors have been represented in almost every field. In fact, Blacks have been responsible for the advancement of major industries. The standard of living enjoyed by this country today would not be possible were it not for the efforts of Black scientists and inventors.

This book will acquaint you with 12 great Black scientists and inventors. Among others, you will meet the "Real McCoy," who kept trains moving without failure and downtime. Jan Matzeliger taught us how to mass-produce shoes. Garrett Morgan brought order to our streets. And, Charles Drew taught us how to effectively save blood for future use and benefit.

What was considered impossible yesterday is common today. This book proves that all things are possible. This book further proves that you should not give up on your ideas and dreams.

EMPAK PUBLISHING COMPANY

"BLACK SCIENTISTS AND INVENTORS"
Published by Empak Enterprises, Inc.
212 East Ohio Street, Chicago, IL 60611
Publisher & Editor: Richard L. Green
Associate Editors: Mildred Johnson, Naurice Roberts,
Joyce Martin
Production: Dickinson & Associates, Inc.
Illustrators: Steve Clay & S. Gaston Dobson

Table of Contents

BENJAMIN BANNEKER
1731-1806

Scientists are thinkers. Sometimes they make things work better. At other times, they discover things totally new. They also like to find new ways of doing things. And, they usually like to work with their hands and with numbers. Benjamin Banneker was such a person.

Banneker was born on November 9, 1731, near Baltimore, Maryland. His father was a freed slave named Robert. His mother was also free. Banneker's father was a hard-working man who owned land and built his own log cabin. He worked hard at clearing the fields and planting tobacco. When young Banneker was big enough, he worked on the family farm.

During Banneker's time, many Black Americans were slaves. They were not allowed to attend school. Instead, they had to work for their slave owner. However, Benjamin Banneker was different. He was born free and taught to read and write by his grandmother. He even went to a nearby country school.

Banneker loved math. In fact, he enjoyed puzzles, games or anything involving mathematics. He also liked history and reading. But, math was his favorite subject. After a day of school and work on the farm, he would read some of his many books. Sometimes, at night, he would often lie on the ground, looking at the stars and studying the heavens.

Once a traveling salesman gave Banneker a pocket watch. He wondered how the watch worked. After taking it apart, he found out. In 1753, with what he had learned, he made a wooden clock. This was the very first wooden clock ever built in the United States. It kept perfect time for over forty years! People came from everywhere to meet the young inventor and see his fine clock.

In 1771, a neighbor talked to Banneker about astronomy. Astronomy is the study of the planets and stars. The neighbor

4

also lent him books, tools, and a table to study on. With this information, Banneker taught himself astronomy.

Because of his interest in astronomy, Banneker decided to write an almanac. This a book with many facts that are helpful to farmers. Almanacs include information about the weather, the planets, the stars, and when to plant crops. Banneker's almanac also included a calendar, recipes, poems, and articles against slavery. Because he was a free man, he wanted other Black people to also be free.

After the death of his parents, Benjamin Banneker lived alone on the family farm. He never married. His three sisters, who lived nearby, would often visit and care for his needs.

One of the most important things that Banneker did was his work in the planning of Washington, D.C. In 1791, he was invited to help survey, or measure, some land. This land later became Washington, D.C., our nation's capital. Banneker also helped design the plans for the capital's streets and buildings.

When the chief surveyor of the Washington project left and returned to France, he took the plans with him. Benjamin Banneker had a very sharp mind. He had remembered every single detail. As a result, Washington, D.C. was built as planned.

In 1792, Banneker returned to his farm. His interest in astronomy was greater than ever before. He immediately began writing other almanacs. He published them for almost ten years. He even sent a letter and a copy of his almanac to Thomas Jefferson. Banneker wanted to prove that Blacks were intelligent, capable of learning, and deserved to be free. Thomas Jefferson agreed! On October 25, 1806, Benjamin Banneker died while doing one of the things he loved most — studying the stars.

TEST YOURSELF

1. What was Banneker's best school subject?
2. Banneker invented something very different. What was it?
3. What is an almanac?
4. What made Banneker different from other slaves at the time?
5. Of all Benjamin Banneker's achievements, which was the most important?
6. Banneker convinced Thomas Jefferson of something very important. What was it?

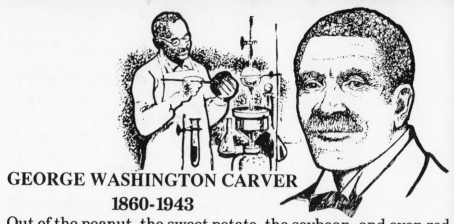

GEORGE WASHINGTON CARVER
1860-1943

Out of the peanut, the sweet potato, the soybean, and even red clay soil, came products which would amaze the world! George Washington Carver, a great Black scientist, made it possible.

Carver was born in Diamond Grove, Missouri, in 1860. George and his mother were slaves on the Moses Carver farm. He was just an infant when he and his mother were stolen by night riders. After a long search, George was found. He was traded back to the Carvers for a race horse. George was a sickly boy. So, he didn't have to do hard work. However, he loved to work in the garden, and he became very interested in plants.

George had a strong desire to seek an education. At the age of ten, he left the Carver farm to attend school in Kansas. To support himself, he worked as a farmhand, a cook, and a laundry helper. He finished high school and tried to enter Highland University. He was refused entry when it was learned that he was Black. Carver was disappointed, but he would not give up! He wanted an education badly. Finally, at the age of 30, Simpson College in Iowa accepted him.

After a year at Simpson, he was accepted at the college now known as Iowa State University. He began his studies in plant and farm science. In 1894, he was the first Black American to graduate from this school. Because he was such a good student, he was made an instructor. Although he taught others, Carver continued to complete his studies with plants and soil at Iowa State. Within two years, he received his Master's degree.

Because of Carver's wonderful work, he was offered many jobs. In 1896, he accepted the invitation of Booker T. Washington to teach at Tuskegee Institute in Alabama. He worked at this famous Black college for the rest of his life. He wanted to help his people.

For many years, the South's only crop was cotton. This made the soil very poor. Carver told farmers that they should first

6

plant peanuts, clover, or peas to make the soil richer. Then they should plant cotton. At first, many farmers did not listen because Carver was Black. However, after they learned of his success with some farmers, they did as he said. The soil grew richer, and the South began to make real progress.

It was not long before Carver was known all over the world. Scientists from other countries visited Carver's lab. Here he made over 300 products from the peanut alone! Instant coffee, milk, peanut butter, face cream, ink, and soaps are just some of the things he created from the peanut. From the sweet potato, he made rubber. From red clay, he made paint dyes.

Even though he was famous, George Washington Carver remained a simple and religious man. He never married. Money and other things did not mean much to him. He gave his entire life savings, over $30,000, to science. He died at Tuskegee on January 5, 1943.

Dr. Carver received many awards in his lifetime. Honors came from other countries as well as the United States. Although Carver received these awards, his life goals never changed. He wanted to make useful products from common things.

There is a Carver Museum at Tuskegee University. Some of his discoveries, collections, and paintings can be seen by the public. Many schools in the U.S. are named in his honor.

This great Black American is recognized as one of the finest scientists the world has ever known. His birthplace in Diamond Grove, Missouri, is a national monument. In 1948, a stamp was issued in his honor. In 1973, he was elected to the New York University Hall of Fame.

TEST YOURSELF

1. What very upsetting event occurred early in Carver's life?
2. What famous Black college employed Carver for most of his life?
3. Why didn't the farmers who had unproductive soil first listen to Carver?
4. Early in his life, what appeared more important to Carver than anything else?
5. Carver's laboratory produced over 300 products and in so doing turned farming around. From what plant were the 300 products derived?
6. Why do you think Carver remained a religious and simple man despite fame and fortune?

CHARLES DREW
1904-1950

Many lives today are saved because blood can be stored until it is needed. Dr. Charles Richard Drew, a Black American scientist, found a way to preserve and store blood. This led to his starting the world's first blood bank.

Charles, the oldest of five children, was born on June 3, 1904, in Washington, D.C. There young Drew attended Stevens Elementary and Dunbar High Schools. At that time, Dunbar prepared more Black American students for college than any other high school in the nation.

As Charles Drew grew up, he learned about segregation. Certain laws kept Blacks and Whites apart. They could not go to the same public places. As a Black American, Drew thought that segregation was unfair.

Drew attended Amherst College in Massachusetts. There he was a star athlete. He played football, ran track, and was on the swimming team. But, this great athlete was denied certain honors because he was Black. This did not stop Charles Drew. He pushed forward and graduated with high honors in 1926.

Although he could work as a teacher or coach, Drew decided on a medical career. In 1928, he entered the McGill University Medical School in Canada. Even though he did not have much money, the young medical student wanted to become a doctor. So, he got a job as a waiter. Working and going to school was difficult.

In 1930, he won a scholarship. His money troubles were over. As a senior, he was one of the top five men in his graduating class. In 1933, Dr. Charles Drew earned his medical degree. While still at McGill University, he developed an interest in the various types of blood. He soon realized this would be his life's work.

At Columbia Hospital, Drew developed a way to preserve blood. His next step was the creation of a blood bank. This was a place where blood could be stored for many months. Soon, hospitals everywhere had a blood bank.

In 1939, Charles Drew married Lenore Robbins of Philadelphia. They had four children. Drew continued to work and study at several hospitals. In 1940, he earned a Doctor of Science in Medicine degree.

When World War II began, Dr. Drew's work was so successful that the British government asked for his help. The blood banks which he set up saved thousands of lives. Then Dr. Drew became the first director of the American Red Cross Blood Bank. After the war, he returned to Europe. He worked with a four-man team to help improve medical care.

Dr. Drew was also a teacher. He taught at Howard University Medical School in Washington, D.C. This famous Black college trains many Blacks in medicine even today. In addition to teaching surgeons, Dr. Drew wrote a number of scientific papers and books.

In 1950, Dr. Drew and three other doctors were on their way to a medical meeting at Tuskegee Institute. Their car overturned, and Dr. Drew was killed at the age of 45. However, his name will live forever in medical history. Schools and hospitals throughout the United States honor him.

TEST YOURSELF

1. What high school prepared more Black students for college?
2. At what point did Drew know what his life's work would be?
3. How did Dr. Drew tragically die?
4. Why was a blood bank so important?
5. How did Charles Drew experience discrimination, first-hand?
6. What well-known agency did Drew first direct?

LLOYD AUGUSTUS HALL
1894-1971

Chemistry is the study of certain substances and the changes that take place when they are combined. A person who studies chemistry is called a chemist. One chemist, a Black American, changed the meat packing industry forever! His name was Lloyd Augustus Hall.

Hall was born in Elgin, Illinois, on June 20, 1894. He was an honor student at East Side High School in Aurora, Illinois. There he developed an interest in chemistry. He did very well in school. He graduated among the top ten students in a class of 125.

Hall received offers to attend some of the nation's best colleges. He selected Northwestern University, which was near his home. There he studied the subjects of drugs and medicine. After graduation, he went on to study at the University of Chicago and the University of Illinois.

In 1916, he was well-prepared to get a job with the Chicago Department of Health. A skillful and hard worker, Lloyd Hall became a senior chemist within a year. Because of his fine work, he went from one high position to another.

Hall became interested in food chemistry. So, he joined Griffith Laboratories as a chief chemist. Again, hard work paid off. He became president of the company in 1922. However, he later gave up this position to become chief chemist and director of research at Griffith. He worked for 37 years before retiring in 1959.

Lloyd Augustus Hall was a brilliant chemist. His work with chemicals and meats changed the entire meat packing industry. He figured out a way to preserve meat. Now meat could stay fresh longer.

Hall didn't stop there. He continued to make new and different discoveries. He developed a way to keep foods free from germs and spoiling. Because of Lloyd Hall, foods not only looked and tasted better but were healthier, too.

The U.S. Army soon learned about this Black American chemist. During World War I, Lloyd Hall was put in charge of powder and explosives. This was a very dangerous job. His job was to make certain that the explosives were made correctly.

There were many problems during the next World War. Again, Hall was there. He helped to solve problems with military food supplies. The food often spoiled and could not be eaten. This smart chemist solved the problem. A form of common table salt was used to preserve foods.

Dr. Lloyd Hall was always willing to share his knowledge with others. He wrote over 50 scientific papers. He also received 105 U.S. and foreign patents. Many companies throughout the world used his methods and learned from his research.

Because of Hall's work with food, he became known as the Food Chemist. He had always been interested in science although it was not a popular subject when he attended school. However, his love of the subject grew as he became older and worked in different companies. His methods of preserving foods is how he is best remembered. He received many special awards and honors. Lloyd Augustus Hall died in 1971.

If you like science, you can learn from studying the works of Lloyd Augustus Hall. Science plays a very important part in our society. Perhaps someday you can add to the progress made by Hall and other great Black American scientists.

TEST YOURSELF

1. Why did Hall select Northwestern University for his first college?
2. What did Hall use to keep military food supplies from spoiling during World War II?
3. What is chemistry?
4. Why was Hall's food preservation method so important to all of us?
5. What did Hall come to be called because of his work?
6. What made Hall's position during World War I so important?

FREDERICK McKINLEY JONES
1892-1961

Years ago, ice was used to keep food fresh while being shipped from one place to another. But the ice often melted and the food spoiled. This problem was solved by a Black American inventor named Frederick McKinley Jones.

Frederick McKinley Jones was born in Cincinnati, Ohio, in 1892. At age nine, he became an orphan. He was sent to Kentucky where he lived with a Catholic priest. There he did odd jobs and went to school through the sixth grade.

When he was 16, Jones returned to Cincinnati to look for work. He liked working with cars, so he was hired as a mechanic. Within three years, he was foreman of the auto shop where he worked.

Frederick Jones quickly became an auto expert. Not only did he fix cars, he built them, too. By the time he was 19, he had built several racing cars. He loved racing. He spent more time at the racetrack than at his job. So, he was fired.

Moving to Hallock, Minnesota, Jones took a job as chief mechanic on a large farm. He wanted to learn more about machinery. He made many trips to the library. This was just before World War I. When war broke out, Jones joined the Army and served overseas as an electrician. He earned the rank of sergeant. After the war, he returned to his home in Hallock.

Jones remained interested in electronics. He spent many hours studying at the library. As before, he learned a great deal. With his new knowledge, he was able to build a radio station transmitter. A transmitter sends signals to radios. He also invented a way to put sound to movies.

Soon, people began to hear about Jones' work. In 1930, Joseph A. Numero, a manufacturer, asked Jones to work for his company. The company made motion picture equipment. Jones produced many inventions. His first patent was for a ticket machine used by movie houses. Before long, Jones and Numero went into business together.

One day, Jones wondered why trucks and trains could not be cooled by electricity. He studied the problem and learned just how to solve it! Soon, he was designing air cooling units for trucks moving food products to market.

Numero and Jones then started another company. This new company made cooling units for trucks, trains, ships, and planes. This made it possible to ship meats, fruits, vegetables, and dairy products very long distances. This had never been done before.

During World War II, cooling units designed by Jones were used by the Army to store blood and medicines. By 1949, their company was making three million dollars a year. Jones received over 60 patents for his inventions. Most of them were for his work on the cooling unit.

Frederick McKinley Jones died in 1961. He rose from an orphan with a sixth grade education to become an expert in refrigeration. His inventions completely changed and improved the food transport industry.

TEST YOURSELF

1. How far did Jones go in school?
2. Why do you think Jones was made foreman of the auto shop where he worked?
3. What is a transmitter?
4. Why was the air cooling unit Jones developed so important?
5. What did Jones invent that is still used at the movie theaters today?
6. What caused Jones to be "self-made"?

PERCY L. JULIAN
1899-1975

Glaucoma is a disease that causes blindness. For years, scientists worked on a cure. Today, there is a cure, thanks to a Black American chemist named Percy Lavon Julian.

Julian was born in Montgomery, Alabama, in 1899. His father was a railroad mail clerk. His mother taught school. After grade school, Julian went to a private Black high school in Montgomery. After high school, he entered DePauw University in Indiana.

Because his high school training was so poor, Percy Julian had to take high school classes along with his college courses. He wanted to do well, so he studied long and hard. His grandfather, a former slave, had lost his right hand as punishment for learning to read. So, the young Julian understood the importance of learning. In 1920, he graduated as the top student in his college class.

Soon Percy Julian began a teaching career. He taught chemistry at Fisk University and Howard University. He also earned a Master's degree from Harvard University in Massachusetts. This degree was in chemistry.

In 1929, Julian went to Europe to obtain more education. He studied in Vienna, Austria, and earned a Ph.D. in 1931. While in Austria, he met Dr. Josef Pikl, who later worked with him. Dr. Julian was asked to return to DePauw University. The dean of the college wanted him to teach chemistry and do research. His friend, Dr. Pikl, went back to DePauw with him.

In the college lab, the two scientists began eye research. They wanted to find a cure for glaucoma. The doctors worked many long hours. They were looking for a certain drug. They tried to produce this drug by combining the right chemicals. Dr. Julian and Dr. Pikl continued working, but they needed money. Their research was very expensive. They needed money for supplies, equipment, chemicals, and salaries. Finally, a

14

foundation gave them the money. A foundation gives money to needy causes. Dr. Julian was pleased that his research could go on for two more years.

Late one night, Dr. Julian and Dr. Pikl found what they were searching for. From the soybean, they discovered the chemical to cure glaucoma. It was done! Praise poured in from all over the world.

The dean of DePauw wanted Dr. Julian to head the chemistry department. But, Dr. Julian didn't get the job because he was Black. Dr. Julian thought this was unfair. Yet, there was nothing he could do. He hoped one day that people would be judged by their ability, not their skin color.

Upset with DePauw, Dr. Julian went to work for the Glidden Paint Company. In 1936, he became its chief chemist and director of research. He continued his work, making products from soybeans. During World War II, he developed a special foam that was used to put out fires. This discovery saved thousands of soldiers' lives.

In the early 1950's, he set up his own labs. He continued to produce drugs to fight many diseases. From the soybean, he developed even more medicines. Some of these drugs were helpful to people who had arthritis and cancer. By 1961, Dr. Julian was a very successful business owner. He later sold his business for over two million dollars!

Dr. Percy Julian received many awards. His honors began in his youth and continued during his lifetime. Because he was a caring Black American, nothing could prevent him from sharing his research with the world. He died in 1975.

TEST YOURSELF

1. How would you describe Julian's upbringing?
2. What plant helped in the discovery of the cure for glaucoma?
3. Why did Dr. Julian and Dr. Pikl need money?
4. What made learning especially important to young Julian?
5. Of all Julian's accomplishments, why was the cure for glaucoma so important?
6. How and when did Julian experience discrimination?

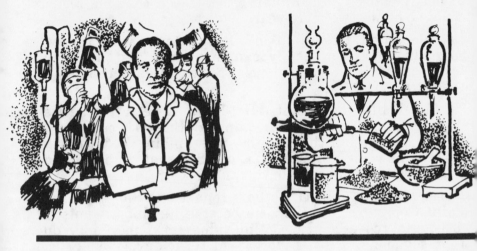

.Who are they?...Why are they famous?

LEWIS HOWARD LATIMER
1848-1928

It is possible for a person to do many things and do them well. This was true of Lewis H. Latimer. He was not only a great inventor, but also a poet, musician, author, artist, and active civil rights spokesman.

Latimer was born in Chelsea, Massachusetts, in 1848, the son of former slaves. He grew up in Boston. In 1865, at age 16, he enlisted in the Union Navy and served as a ship's cabin boy. After the Civil War, he returned to Boston, looking for work.

Lewis had a talent for mechanical drawing and painting. Because of these skills, he took a job with a drafting company. There he became interested in this special kind of drawing. He bought a set of used drafting tools and borrowed several library books. He wanted to learn more about drafting.

After a while, Latimer started drafting on his own. He then asked if he could make some drawings for the company. His work was amazing! Later, he became chief draftsman. He worked for this company eleven years.

During the late 1870's, Lewis Latimer married Mary Wilson. They had two daughters. He loved his wife very much and wrote poems to honor her. His work as a draftsman was also very important to him.

Latimer's job was near a school where Alexander Graham Bell taught deaf people. Bell was trying to invent a machine to help deaf people hear. What Bell invented was the telephone, and he needed to get a patent. A patent is a government paper giving the inventor certain rights. Then the invention belongs only to him. Alexander Graham Bell asked Latimer to help him. Latimer made the drawings and Bell received the patent in 1876.

Soon, Latimer began to work on his own inventions. At the same time, he started thinking about electricity. Because he knew that electricity would be important in the future, he read and studied about it. In 1880, he went to work as a draftsman for an electrical company in Connecticut. A year later, he received a patent for an electric lamp.

In 1882, Latimer received another important patent. His invention was the making of carbon filaments. The filament is a key part of the light bulb. When electricity passes through the filament, it makes the light bulb glow. Latimer's invention made the light bulb safer, last longer, and shine brighter.

Latimer was soon asked to put improved street lights in New York City and Philadelphia. Next, he went to Canada and England to do the same work. While in England, Latimer was also in charge of a factory that made light bulbs.

In 1884, Thomas Edison, a famous White scientist, called. This was an important time in Latimer's life. He was to work with the Edison Pioneers. This was a special group of inventors, electricians, and scientists. Latimer became one of the most important of all the pioneers. He was the only Black American. In 1890, Latimer wrote an important book on electric lighting.

Lewis Latimer died in 1928. Today, we see thousands of lights shining throughout the cities of America and around the world. For this, we should remember Lewis Latimer.

TEST YOURSELF

1. Why did Latimer take a job with a drafting company?
2. How did Latimer meet Alexander Graham Bell?
3. What is a patent?
4. Why was Latimer's invention of the carbon filament important to all of us?
5. Latimer's work with the Edison Pioneers was very important. What made this work even more special?
6. Why did Latimer begin to work on his own inventions after working with Bell?

JOSEPH LEE
1849-1905

Joseph Lee was born in Charleston, South Carolina, in 1849. As a young boy, he worked in a bakery. There he learned to make bread. He had various jobs, making and serving food. Lee soon decided this is what he wanted to do for a living. He wanted to become Master Chef.

Joseph Lee was quite good at his work. By the late 1800's, he owned the Woodland Park Hotel in Newton, Massachusetts. One day, he watched as his cooks threw away stale bread. Lee knew this was a waste. He also knew that bread crumbs could be used for cooking certain dishes. So, he decided to invent a bread crumb machine.

Lee's machine would grind stale bread into crumbs. The crumbs were then used in dressing for chicken, pork chops, fish, clams, oysters and other foods. His hotel customers liked the new dishes. The machine was a success!

Lee received a patent for his bread crumb machine in 1895. He then sold his patent to a large company. Soon the bread crumb machine was an important piece of equipment in the best hotels and restaurants. Lee's machine became very popular. And he became famous almost overnight. He also made a lot of money from his bread crumb machine.

Lee got another idea. If he could make a bread crumb machine, then why not a machine for making bread? He went to work! The Lee Bread Making Machine was born. It mixed the ingredients and kneaded, or stretched, the dough much faster and better than a baker. It made hundreds of loaves daily. When bread was made by hand, it took nearly a dozen men to make the same number of loaves. The machine made better bread. The bread was whiter, finer in texture, and softer.

By now, he had gained a great reputation. He was a well-known chef and inventor. In 1902, he opened the Lee Catering Company. His company cooked and delivered food. Many

20

wealthy people wanted him to cook for them. Like his machines, his company was also successful. During the summer, Lee operated a fancy restaurant by the seashore. It was well known for its excellent food.

Joseph Lee was a master chef, inventor, and businessman. The baking industry was never the same after his bread machines were invented. Lee's insight and talent contributed greatly to the growth of the food industry worldwide. He died around 1905.

TEST YOURSELF

1. How did Lee's bread making machine improve the bread making process?
2. What business did Lee open in 1902?
3. What and where was the hotel Lee owned?
4. What made Lee think about the waste in the kitchen of his hotel?
5. How did Lee's bread crumb machine add to a restaurant's menu?
6. How did Lee become so well known?

JAN EARNST MATZELIGER
1852-1889

Take a look at your shoes. Ever wonder how they are made? It once took a factory ten hours to make fifty pairs. A Black American, Jan Matzeliger, made it possible to turn out hundreds of shoes a day with his invention.

Matzeliger was born on September 15, 1852, in South America. His mother was Black and his father was a White engineer from Holland. At the age of ten, young Matzeliger was sent to work in a machine shop. He soon discovered that he worked well with his hands and machines.

When he was 19, Matzeliger went to sea for two years. He left the ship and spent a few years doing odd jobs in Philadelphia. In 1876, he moved to Boston and then to Lynn, Massachusetts. He would spend the rest of his life in this small town.

When Matzeliger went to Lynn, he did not speak English very well. He worked in a shoe factory and went to school in the evening. The shoemaker made great progress. He practiced speaking English in his free time. He knew it was important to learn English. He also understood that it was important to learn other subjects. So, he gathered different kinds of books for his library. He liked books on science and machinery. He taught himself many things just by reading.

Lynn, Massachusetts was the shoe making capital of the world. In those early days, it was very hard to sew the sole (bottom) to the upper part of the shoe. This had to be done by hand. No one thought a machine could be invented to do this work.

This was a great challenge for Jan Matzeliger. He worked on the problem for several years. In the fall of 1880, his first "Lasting Machine" was invented. It was made of wire, wood, and cigar boxes. Even so, he received a patent.

Matzeliger wanted to build a better model, but he needed money to make the changes. Some people tried to buy his patent from him for very little money. He turned down their offers and kept searching. Finally, he found two investors. Investors often spend money on good ideas.

On May 29, 1885, the public saw the first testing of the "Lasting Machine." It made 75 pair of shoes that day. Everyone saw that Matzeliger's machine would change the entire shoe industry forever. Shoes could now be made much cheaper and faster. Also, more people could afford to buy them.

Although in poor health, Matzeliger worked on other inventions. He received more patents. One of his machines made a complete shoe! Matzeliger's health continued to fail. He died on August 24, 1889, at the age of 37. He never married.

Following his death, Matzeliger was awarded the Gold Medal and Diploma in 1901. In later years, a statue was built in his honor in Lynn, Massachusetts.

Now, take another look at your shoes. Just think, mass-produced shoes were made possible by the inventions of a great Black American.

TEST YOURSELF

1. Why didn't Matzeliger speak English well?
2. Where was the shoe-making capital of the world?
3. What is an investor?
4. How did Matzeliger's "Lasting Machine" change the shoe in industry?
5. Why do you think Matzeliger thought it was so important to learn English?
6. What was Matzeliger's greatest challenge in his work?

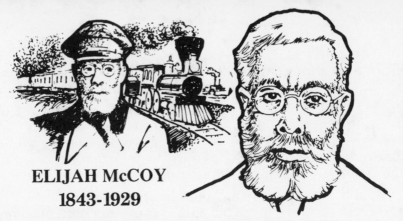

ELIJAH McCOY
1843-1929

Have you ever heard of the saying, "the Real McCoy?" It means something that is new or original. It also means something that is very good! This saying comes from an invention by a Black American. His name was Elijah McCoy.

McCoy was born in Ontario, Canada, in 1843. He was the third of twelve children. His parents, George and Mildred McCoy, were runaway slaves from Kentucky. The family later moved back to the United Sates and settled in Michigan, where Elijah attended grade school.

Young McCoy loved math and decided early to become an engineer. An engineer operates, builds, and fixes machines. McCoy's father was a carpenter who believed in education. He sent his son, at the age of 15, to study engineering in Scotland. Years later, Elijah McCoy returned to the United States.

McCoy was well-trained, educated, and eager to begin work as an engineer. However, no one would hire a Black engineer. McCoy kept trying to find a job in his field. Unable to do so, he accepted a job as a fireman with the railroad.

One of McCoy's duties was to oil the moving parts on the train engine. Machinery must be oiled. If not, the moving parts will wear out. Elijah McCoy felt that it was a waste of time and money to stop a train or shut down a machine just to oil it. So, in 1870, he started the Elijah McCoy Manufacturing Company in Detroit, Michigan. He wanted to work on his ideas to solve the problem.

By 1872, McCoy had invented and patented an automatic lubricator. He called it the "lubricator cup." It was also known as the "drip cup." His invention made it possible for oil to flow or drip on the moving parts of a machine. This allowed machines to run without being stopped.

McCoy's valuable invention saved time, energy and money. Factories everywhere began to use it. Elijah McCoy also invented a lubricator cup for the steam engine. Soon all railroads and steamships were also using his invention. The "lubricator cup" made McCoy famous.

McCoy kept thinking of new ways to improve the oiling of machinery. He received many patents for his inventions. Many of his patents were sold because he needed money to continue his work.

Railroad and factory inspectors, when checking a new piece of machinery, would ask, "Is it the real McCoy?" They wanted to know if it had the McCoy lubricator. People continue to say, "the real McCoy" even today. Although Elijah McCoy was a fine engineer and inventor, some companies did not want to use his lubricator cup because it was invented by a Black man.

Elijah McCoy became known as a great engineer and inventor throughout the world. He often talked to young Black children. He encouraged them to work hard, study, and to think.

McCoy continued to improve upon his invention of the lubricator cup. No piece of large machinery was said to be complete unless it used this invention. He also received patents for an ironing table, lawn sprinkler and other inventions. In all, McCoy received over 50 patents.

Elijah J. McCoy lived to be nearly ninety years old. He died in Detroit, Michigan, in 1929. His outstanding work as an inventor helped to improve the whole world.

TEST YOURSELF

1. What is another name for the "lubricator cup?"
2. McCoy invented two very useful household items. What were they?
3. McCoy's love of this subject was an early sign he'd be a good engineer. What was the subject?
4. Why was Elijah McCoy's invention so important to modern industry?
5. Why was McCoy unable to find a job in his field?
6. What is the meaning of the saying "the real McCoy?"

GARRETT A. MORGAN
1875-1963

Can you imagine what the streets would be like if there were no traffic signals? Well, a Black American, named Garrett A. Morgan, solved this problem.

Garrett A. Morgan was born in Paris, Kentucky, on March 4, 1875. He was the seventh of eleven children born to Elizabeth and Sydney Morgan. Garrett went to grade school, but no further. He stopped after the fifth grade at the age of 14. Then he left home, went to Cincinnati, Ohio, and worked as a handyman. There were not many jobs available for him, so he moved to Cleveland. Morgan stayed there for life.

Morgan got a job as a sewing machine repairman without knowing how to fix them. However, he quickly learned. Soon, he started his own sewing machine business. In fact, his first invention was a belt fastener for sewing machines. He sold his invention in 1901 for $50.00.

In 1909, Morgan wanted a larger company, so he opened a tailoring shop. In a short time, he had 32 workers. They made dresses, suits, and coats. In one year, he earned enough money to buy a home for his wife, Mary Anne. He was also able to send for his mother.

Morgan became quite successful. He liked the idea of inventing new and different machines. But, his next invention was not a machine. Around 1913, he discovered a mixture that made hair straight. This was the first product of the G.A. Morgan Hair Refining Company. His new company provided money for him to continue with other inventions.

His next invention was the safety hood, later known as the gas mask. Firemen were being overcome by fumes and thick smoke when entering burning buildings. The hood allowed a fireman to breathe freely through a tube attached to it. There was no fear of breathing smoke or poison gas. The safety hood was patented in 1914. During the same year, Morgan received a gold medal for his invention.

On July 25, 1916, Morgan's gas mask was put to a real test. Following an explosion, men were trapped in a underground tunnel by a deadly gas. Using his gas masks, Morgan and his brother saved many lives. For their rescue, he received many medals and awards. The gas mask was used on the battlefield during World War I. It saved many lives. In fact, the gas mask continues to save lives even today.

The idea for the traffic light came after Morgan saw an accident at a street crossing. Morgan worked on his idea for a long time. He wanted to do something to help stop accidents. He also wanted to help traffic move better. In 1913, he received a patent on his traffic signal. Today, traffic lights are used all over the world.

During the 1920's, Morgan started a newspaper known as the *Cleveland Call*. It reported news on Black Americans. It is still being printed and has thousands of readers. Today, the newspaper is known as the *Cleveland Call and Post*.

Morgan proved that the wise use of intelligence could benefit the lives of many people. Even today, his inventions remind us of his genius. Garrett A. Morgan died at the age of 88, in 1963.

TEST YOURSELF

1. What is interesting about Morgan's place of birth?
2. Why do you think Morgan stopped school after the fifth grade?
3. Why do you think Morgan was able to get a job as a sewing machine repairman when he didn't know how to fix sewing machines?
4. What did Morgan purchase early in his career that showed he had great success for the times?
5. In terms of safety, what were Morgan's most important inventions?
6. What was Morgan's reason for inventing the traffic light?

NORBERT RILLIEUX
1806-1894

The next time you scoop up a spoonful of sugar, take a good look at it. Those are tiny sugar crystals that you see. A Black American invented and produced the modern way of making sugar. His name was Norbert Rillieux.

Rillieux was born on a plantation in New Orleans, Louisiana, on March 17, 1806. His father was Vincent Rillieux, a rich slave owner and engineer. His mother, Constant Vivant, was a slave. The little boy was adopted by his father. This was very unusual. Many slavemasters did not recognize or even want their children.

As the free son of a White planter, young Rillieux was special. He went to the best schools in New Orleans. He even studied in Paris and became an engineer. At age 24, he became a teacher at his college.

While teaching, he wrote scientific papers on the steam engine that drew attention to his work. Scientists all over Europe knew about this intelligent Black man. The young scientist took time out to marry his wife, Emily. However, he and his wife Emily did not have a family. In 1834, they returned to New Orleans.

Having grown up on his father's sugar plantation, Rillieux knew how sugar cane was turned into table syrup and sugar. This process was expensive and even dangerous. Slaves had to carry boiling sugar cane juice from one huge kettle to another. They worked hard and were often burned by the hot liquid. Rillieux believed there was a better and safer way to make refined, or pure, sugar.

While in Paris, Rillieux had worked on methods to remove moisture from sugar. This he did by a heating and drying process called evaporation. This later led to his first patent in 1843. However, there were problems with his invention. But,

28

Norbert Rillieux worked long, hard years to solve them. He believed in himself and what he was doing.

In 1846, Rillieux received another patent for the improvement on his invention. Sugar growers could now mass-produce sugar. It could be made better and cheaper. His invention changed the entire sugar industry worldwide. His invention process also led to the making of many other products.

Another invention of Rillieux's was his method to rid New Orleans of its sewage problem. This sewage problem caused mosquitoes, which carried Yellow Fever. Thousands of people died as a result. The city would not accept a Black man's plan for killing the mosquitoes. However, years later, the city did accept a similar plan by a group of Whites. Upset, Rillieux decided to leave New Orleans and go back to Paris in 1854. He never returned.

Norbert Rillieux died in Paris at the age of 88 on October 8, 1894. More than 30 years later, a worldwide movement was started to honor him. It began in Holland and spread to include every sugar growing country in the world.

This great inventor was often saddened during his lifetime because of the unfair treatment of his people. Yet, his work as a chemical engineer was the greatest ever done for the sugar industry. It was also tremendous work by a Black American.

When we use sugar, let us not forget Norbert Rillieux. He was the great inventor who made life sweeter for us all.

TEST YOURSELF

1. What saddened Rillieux more than anything in his life?
2. What is evaporation?
3. Why was Rillieux's plan for solving the New Orleans sewage problem rejected?
4. What was so unusual about Rillieux's father?
5. What made Rillieux want to develop a better way to make sugar?
6. What other very important method did Rillieux develop?

GLOSSARY

arthritis	A disease causing pain and swelling of a joint or joints in the body.
benefit	Anything which is for the good of a person or thing.
brilliant	Shining brightly; very smart.
cancer	A very harmful growth in or on the body.
capable	Able; having ability or power.
carbon	An element found in coal, oil, and other substances.
chemistry	Science that deals with the elements, their changes, and the laws under which they act.
crystal	A clear and transparent substance.
drafting	Drawing of plans or designs from which buildings and machines are made.
electrician	Person who installs or repairs electric wiring, lights, etc.
electricity	Form of energy which can produce light, heat, motion, etc.
electronics	Study of the production, flow, motion, and use of electrons.
engineer	Person who takes care of or runs engines.
equipment	Supplies and other things needed to do something.
expert	Person who knows a great deal about some special thing.
explosives	A substance which blows up with a loud noise and great force.
filament	A very fine thread or wire.
foreman	Person in charge of a group of workers or of some part of a factory.
genius	Very great power of mind and ability.
goal	Something for which an effort is made; something wanted.
handyman	Person who can do many odd jobs.
industry	A business.
insight	Power of understanding people and things.
instructor	Teacher.
intelligent	Able to learn and know; quick to understand.
inventor	Person who makes up things for the first time.

kettle	A metal pot for boiling liquids, cooking fruits, etc.
lubricator	A device which applies oil to machines.
machinery	Group of fixed and moving parts for doing work; machine.
mass-produced	Making of goods in large numbers.
master chef	A cook who has been trained at a special school and is highly respected for his skill.
mechanic	Worker who uses tools, especially one who repairs machines.
mechanical drawing	Drawing of machines, tools, etc., done to exact scale with rulers, compasses, etc.
moisture	Slight wetness.
monument	Something, often a statue, to honor a person or event.
orphan	A child whose parents are dead.
patent	A legal paper which gives a person or company sole rights to make, use, or sell a new intention.
plan	Way of making or doing something that has been worked out beforehand.
progress	A moving forward or going ahead; improvement.
recognize	To know again; to be accepted.
reputation	What people say and think about the goodness of another person.
research	A careful hunting for facts or truth.
scholarship	Money or other aid given to help a student continue his studies.
segregation	Keeping one group or race apart from another in housing, schools, jobs, etc.
sergeant	An officer ranking next above a corporal in the army.
sugar cane	A very tall grass with a strong stem which is the main source of sugar.
talent	Special natural ability to do something.
transport	Carry from one place to another.
tremendous	Very great.
Yellow Fever	A disease of warm places given by the bite of certain mosquitoes, causing high fever, and turning the skin yellow.

end to: Empak Publishing Company, 212 E. Ohio St., Suite 300, Chicago, IL 60611—Phone: (312) 642-8364

Name _____

Affiliation _____

Address _____
P. O. Box numbers not accepted, street address must appear.

City _____ State _____ Zip _____

Phone# (_____)_____ Date _____

thod Of Payment Enclosed:　　( ) Check　　　( ) Money Order　　　( ) Purchase Order

Prices effective 10/1/93 thru 8/31/94

ADVANCED LEVEL

uantity	ISBN #	Title Description	Unit Price	Total Price
	0-9616156-0-5	"A Salute to Historic Black Women"		
	0-9616156-1-3	"A Salute to Black Scientists & Inventors"		
	0-9616156-2-1	"A Salute to Black Pioneers"		
	0-9616156-3-X	"A Salute to Black Civil Rights Leaders"		
	0-9616156-4-8	"A Salute to Historic Black Abolitionists"		
	0-9616156-5-6	"A Salute to Historic African Kings & Queens"		
	0-9616156-6-4	"A Salute to Historic Black Firsts"		
	0-9616156-7-2	"A Salute to Historic Blacks in the Arts"		
	0-9616156-8-0	"A Salute to Blacks in the Federal Government"		
	0-922162-00-X	"A Salute to Historic Black Educators"		

INTERMEDIATE LEVEL

	0-922162-75-1	"Historic Black Women"		
	0-922162-76-X	"Black Scientists & Inventors"		
	0-922162-77-8	"Historic Black Pioneers"		
	0-922162-78-6	"Black Civil Rights Leaders"		
	0-922162-80-8	"Historic Black Abolitionists"		
	0-922162-81-6	"Historic African Kings & Queens"		
	0-922162-82-4	"Historic Black Firsts"		
	0-922162-83-2	"Historic Blacks in the Arts"		
	0-922162-84-0	"Blacks in the Federal Government"		
	0-922162-85-9	"Historic Black Educators"		

Total Books		❸ Subtotal	
	SEE ABOVE CHART ▷	❹ IL Residents add 8.75% Sales Tax	
		❺ Shipping & Handling	
GRADE LEVEL: 4th, 5th, 6th		❻ Total	

KEY STEPS IN ORDERING
❶ Establish quantity needs.　❹ Add tax, if applicable.
❷ Determine book unit price.　❺ Add shipping & handling.
❸ Determine total cost.　❻ Total amount.

BOOK PRICING • QUANTITY DISCOUNTS
❶ Quantity Ordered　❷ Unit Price
1-49　　$2.09
50 +　　$1.77

❺ SHIPPING AND HANDLING
Order Total	Add
Under $5.00	$1.50
$5.01-$15.00	$3.00
$15.01-$35.00	$4.50
$35.01-$75.00	$7.00
$75.01-$200.00	10%
Over $201.00	6%

In addition to the above charges, U.S. territories, HI & AK, add $2.00. Canada & Mexico, add $5.00. Other outside U.S., add $20.00.